# The Stone Garden

Also by Diane Fahey:

*Voices from the Honeycomb*
*Metamorphoses*
*Turning the Hourglass*
*Mayflies in Amber*
*The Body in Time*
*Listening to a Far Sea*
*The Sixth Swan*
*Sea Wall and River Light*
*Winter Solstice*
*The Mystery of Rosa Morland*
*The Wing Collection: New & Selected Poems*

# The Stone Garden
*Poems from Clare*

## Diane Fahey

Clouds of Magellan | Melbourne

ISBN: 978-0-9874037-3-5

Cover image: hEireann, at en.wikipedia
Author photo: Irena Zdanowicz
Cover design by G Thompson

## Acknowledgements

Special thanks to Linda Saunders for her
companionship and insight during many journeys
through County Clare.

For their comments on the poems, warm and
grateful thanks to Linda, and to Rosemary Blake,
Sandy Fitts, Miriel Lenore, Angela Livingstone,
Robyn Rowland and Irena Zdanowicz.

To my publisher, Gordon Thompson, my cordial
thanks and appreciation.

\*

*The Stone Garden* is written in tanka, the five-line Japanese
lyric form, the first and third of its lines having five
syllables, the others, seven.

# Contents

# I

# Hill Cottage

*At Ballinruan*

The cottage

sits in a meadow:
silvered hemlock, buttercups,
sorrel... To the north,
Burren country; south, east, west,
pastureland, streams, clumped oaks, ash.




Settling in

One window offers
fields, hills, stretching to the coast.
By the road, bindweed,
cranesbill, yellow irises.
In the hedge, nesting whitethroats.

Blue house, the next hill

Through unlit windows
I glimpse a wall, east-facing,
with twin portraits of
ambered gold; from my own dusk
watch the sky grow wide, tall, deep.




Early

Dolmens in the clouds.
On high wires, the revellers –
whitethroats, goldfinches –
sing against hills (mauve or green,
who could say), sandstone mountains.

From the farmer

high on his tractor
each morning, a wave – stronger,
so I thought, after
our first exchange of words steeped in
the holy water of silence.

Morning walk

Always a welcome
in the wild places, some lone
warbler – a chiffchaff
perhaps – countering an oak's
wet sigh above peaty gulfs.

The unwilling white

of bramble-flowers,
clover, hemlock, today's sky,
mixed with hedgerow-jewels:
honeysuckle, vetch, foxglove;
wild strawberries on the tongue.


The heat, at last

Wrens flower from hedges,
dart in charmed spurts through air's
temple. Chaffinches
dip with closed wings, touch unseen
stones across unseen waters.

Meadow pipit

His twinned note plaintive:
*I'm here: but where is that?* Soon,
song-flights – voice quickened
in the climb, slowing as he
parachutes on half-spread wings.


Goldfinches at noon

As if there were not
enough gold in this meadow
they bounce over it,
pause among the buttercups
to feast on dark-rose seedheads.

Utterance

Beside the hill road
brambled nests, wrens, bumble bees;
a stream. At the turn,
water flows from a spout wreathed
in leaves, buds: mouth of a god.


Hill view

Down the tilted field
the cows, as with one mind,
run with governed speed,
their eyes calm, loose-muscled bulk
flowing over epic bones.

A surmise of ravens

hovers on washed pearl,
swoops on green rows already
seeded with black. *Rain
tomorrow.* wielding pitchforks
the men labour till nightfall.




Last night

the lamp off, we watched
clouds, brute black barges drifting
on ten o'clock light –
gold at melting point. No moon.
An owl's cry. Summer gothic.

Summer

Breath by breath, taking,
surrendering life, I dwell
in the midst of wild
grasses; fields stripped, striped; spring-coiled
foxes; the sough of black wings.

# II

# At Dromore Wood

Dromore Wood

Each tree a presence
revealing, sharing its power;
a lived story of
ringed heartwood, of soundlessly
uttered leaves – wind-words, rain-words.


Sunlit path

The glint of brimstones,
perhaps. Beneath us, roots search.
The highest boughs sweep
monumental wisps into
blue, leaf-edged blue. The wind stops.

Glade

Bees, willow warblers;
sun-ignited orchids, ling;
a fritillary
dithering... Ash, oak and lime
quiver, Aeolian.


Island walk

We entered groves of
tinsel leaves set on fire by
cool winds. Meadow browns
sudden above gorse. From shade
the stone seat beckoned to us.

Bird's-nest orchid

A tiny steeple
climbed by derelict brown blooms
tinged with ash, honey,
it wears the charisma of
rarity; gone the next day.


Rest

Silence does its work.
Like a slowly raised vessel
in a lock, I float
on a brimming plane of light,
poised for the fresh glide forward.

Woodland trail

Lost, yes, but that meant
I caught the lake by surprise –
its sequestered gleam;
the way it was polishing
the smooth grey stones it has loved.


Dromore Lough

Reeds in italics.
Water scripted with wind-song.
In unghostly white
swans hold sway among lilies
(softly furled, marmoreal).

Great crested grebes

Three stripy chicks feed
on the white feathers she plucks;
slip at will from their
winged island to swim above
shrimps, fish, frogs; climb back on board.


Photograph

We superimpose
our density on beauty.
My amateur smile
against the scuffed lough's sky-flare.
I tune my pulse to the wind.

By the lake

Lie in the grass, place
dead insects upon your heart.
Without touching you
those questing swallows would dive,
clear that burden in seconds.




Speeding away

The ranger's anguish
at food wrappings in his Eden.
He shows us the rare
orchid. The cry of a dog
forced to jump into a car boot.

Tableau, visitors' centre

Their counterparts breathe
outside – squirrel, pine marten;
the long-eared owl
whose eyes ask black-and-gold questions
only its claws can answer.


Curlew

Because its call came
as we were speaking of it,
the sound passed through us
the more keenly, vibrantly:
like a koan unfolding.

Mallard

A green-headed drake
flies to break the record books –
dividing the sky's
great lough, heralding day's end:
the hills greener now; closer.

# III

# The stone garden

Poulnabrone portal tomb

*Used for fewer than 30 burials between 3800 and 3200 BC,*
*this tomb was described by its excavator, Ann Lynch, as 'a*
*place for the special dead'.*

Gateway and shelter
for the special dead, amid
multitudes of stones
once under sea; some shield
the unmapped dead of millennia.


The cliffs at Poulsallagh

Count the Burren's stones –
count leaves in a summer wood.
Not god-like, not small,
you walk on pavements the grey
of gull wings, pooled with blown spray.

These vast platforms

leave you alone with
the clouds' furled secrets, slowly
giving themselves away;
wind-poised hawks; the Atlantic,
fallow then whitely fertile.

Stone gardens

*In the Burren a very high degree of light is achieved by
reflections from the sea and from the limestone.*
— Clare County Library website

Rain-scoured, polished by
glaciers, these slabs give back
the watery light.
Between them: hart's-tongue ferns, moss,
blue gentians, bloody cranesbill.

Gryke

From its lush covert
a dove flies through stone lips, whirrs
upward, its plumage
bearing the karst's earthen grey
into an aureoled sun.


Ice-gifts, wind-gifts

Arctic-alpine seeds
mingle with seeds from the South,
take root in gouged stones;
archives of filigree life
compact as bottle-gardens.

Along hill terraces

white mountain avens,
hoary rockrose, the orchids,
the gentians, flow with
and resist the wind; thrive on
sea mist, rain of any kind.


Coast walk

The rain seems to have
breath, mind, a body, as it
stalks us, leans on us,
scouts the stony path ahead,
hurries down to meet the waves.

Forced stop

Does the soul love grey?
At one with the stone shore,
a misted sea, rain
fills the space between two hills.
We wait, daunted, thrilled, silent.

The wind knows it all

– how fruit, not-quite-ripe,
resists the plucking hand; how
stone is a locked door
yet will accept tiny gifts,
love them, rive itself for them.

Panic attack, the Cliffs of Moher

A strong hand saved me
once, from the long drop. Now wave-
imprinted slate rims
this cliff – above stacked time; gulls,
puffins on shelves; sea thrift, grass.

At the Cliffs of Moher

*Every year up to 30,000 pairs of seabirds breed here.*

Would I were on board
a gannet-trailed boat, reading
through shifting haze this
unscrolled text: a road for birds;
limed honeycomb of new life.

Spotlight, Aillwee Cave

In slippery dusk
a waterfall tricked into
gaunt brightness; needles
splay out, prick walls already
sluiced, gelid with would-be drops.

At Aillwee Cave

*Bears died out in Ireland a thousand years ago.*

A soft-edged oval:
the bear bed. I am held by
the same deep dark, earthed,
imagining that long sleep,
the heart in its breathing cage.

In a mountain quarry

ringed by pines... Below,
a scoop of Clare: storied earth,
unstoppable green.
Boulders grow through streams, hillsides;
pebbles and grass blades marry.

# IV

# In transit

Watcher
*Deer farm, the Mid Clare Way*

Only her ears move –
as I move, it seems. She rests
as if gathering
the great silence of the earth,
this woodland, into herself.


Hill ascent

On magical thighs
the hare, eyeing us, stood tall;
lumbered up the hill
like an oddly sprung carriage;
turned to gaze; then swift away.

Conversation on a hillside

Tell an inch of your
story, throw across that gulf,
a bridge; see calm-eyed
scepticism deepen or
dissolve. Paths in wind-blown grass.

Giving way

The scrape of hedges.
My sacrificial braking.
Fingers on a wheel
raised in thanks, or not. Pincered
nerves killing dreams of sweet calm.

June

Toyed with by weather,
its miserly, shiftless ways,
we long for dazzle –
days like invisible cloaks
lifted by sea winds; soaring.

Navigator

The map misread but
always we end up somewhere...
This castle, this shore:
the mesmeric wheeling of
terns – their work the wildest play.

Apparition

Over summer fields
a shadow in particles –
corvids heading east,
those many eyes scanning for
bodies in wind-fanned grasses.




A kestrel

finessing stillness.
Behind it, Atlantic winds
collide with mountains;
riffle through beech forests; nudge
dark-heeled clouds creamy with light.

Bird of prey centre

I find the cages.
All are empty except for
that prince tethered to
a stake. A gaze that could span
mountains; wings that could cross them.

Oak tree
*A friend's story*

Sometimes the silence
of that falcon visits me –
'perched high, jesses loose';
soul-pierced by coercion, by
gift-bearing hands. *Glove; hood; meat.*

Sunset

A hawk cuts hilltop
oaks from their shadow: starlings
lift and whirl; unspool;
billow in ghost shapes. Sky-wide
sifts of jet veil coral-red.


At the Fahy Graveyard

I'm told the Faheys
came from this place, farmed strongholds
of green. New names, graves,
beside the nameless headstones.
The half-wall of an old church.

## At a Famine Graveyard

*Three times when speech is better than silence: when urging a
king to battle, when reciting a well turned line of poetry, when
giving due praise.*
     — from 'Triads', Ninth century Irish poem

Three times when silence
is better than speech: holding
new life; letting sea waves
slice through you; beholding
a slope sown with the Hunger's dead.


## On Scattery Island
*Among the monastic ruins*

The coast in clear view —
but they had the wild spaces,
the tall seas, needed
to quell the mind. Winds flailed, keened.
Their peace, hardwon, took root here.

Church concert, Crusheen
*The music of Martin Hayes*

On foot-worn marble
he outfiddles the Devil.
The listening body
is stored with a composite
silence. Down the nave, one breath.

# V

# Encounters

## B&B

She took against me,
changed her mind; spoke of men who'd
watched pornography
on her computer. We talked
of merlins, terns; parted friends.


Separate tables

Full Irish breakfast;
partial consciousness. Slowly
surfacing, I ask:
*How does the morning find you?*
His guess: *Largely by accident.*

Morning tea

One who might seem to
know little, knows everything.
In the bakery
blunt questions, my life taken
account of. A sober warmth.


Afternoon tea

It tinctures the air
of the chatty, chaotic
tea shop – the half-smile
of the Polish girl wiping
glass with her unhappiness.

*I knew Hélder Câmara*

Workmen from Brazil
wait calmly. The young woman
there to support them
warms to my friend's words; they talk
across countries, the decades.

Too late to step back

from this radial
culture. In Ennis, in Gort,
internet shops with
Chileans, a Moroccan,
maintaining the connections.

This Ireland

Money comes; it goes.
Consequences. The bereft,
the bitter. Yet life
remains a crafted story;
wit waits on the glide of words.




After the funeral

the churchyard fills with
characters from Ann Enright:
heart-rich or heart-poor;
lost until further notice.
The wild spenders. The keepers.

Orthodoxy
*The price of certainty*

My own past, I see,
haunts others: this wordless youth,
stalked by sadness, fear.
The lies have been busy with him
filling mind, heart, with dried blood.

In crowded streets

I can pick them out,
the once-broken with their ill-
fitting happiness,
think of blackbirds, those crouched spurts
through gardens mulched with surprise.

Charity shop

*She makes the finest*
*cup of tea you'll ever taste!* —
the woman who runs
this bright, musty shop, who lives
to fill cold, needy spaces.


Shopkeeper

A two-euro shop
crammed to the roof. Her light words,
that patient clear gaze.
She'll decide soon enough if
you are a stranger, or not.

Reading in the dark
*Power outage*

No torches in stock.
*We don't have much call for them*
*this time of the year.*
Summer nights are shorter, true.
Sleepless, I watched the white stars.

The best shop in the world
or
This Babel will never fall

With sweet abandon
a girl stacks goods on skewed shelves
that harbour the rare,
the rejected – all held in trust
by the oral tradition.

A different world
*Long-haul bus driver*

*I was a child bride!*
he tells a long-lost school friend.
Later, not joking,
he says, at my fraught return,
*Did you think I'd leave without you?*


Kindness

– so often crushed by
self-interest – thrives here, present
in the air, the eyes;
the benefit of the doubt
waiting before you arrive.

Around the table

I sense misgivings
in the priest off to Africa.
Some have travelled hours
to greet him. We're all grounded
by the spacious warmth, the talk.


Woman in a doorway

As if she'd stepped back
from life; the shut door behind.
*A fine day, thank God.*
Her eyes, her smile, know the way
of things. So quiet in her skin.

Tourist office
*At Scarriff, near Lough Derg*

The fresh-eyed young man
stood outside with us. Even
his fingers were tall.
*Two miles. Down that road. A lough.*
*I think you'd like it.* We did.

# VI

# At Lough Derg

Lunch at Lough Derg

The holy island
misted then clear. Water-shine.
Lace-headed grasses.
Whitethroats, blackcaps, making free
with a thornbush. Sandwiches.

From the pier

I can see, against
a wake of chipped quartz, the midge
swiped by a wagtail;
frisson of a lily pad
dry inside its rim of light.

Lakeside

In glorious browns
the mallards swim by... Red-eyed
hisses, the snow glare
of towering wings; all curves,
his dreamboat cygnets, pale-taupe.


Tern

At each exactly
timed, exquisitely angled
entry, clouds struggle
against drowning, the pull of
a deep, deep sky. *Lift. Repeat.*

*Inis Cealtra*

*In the Sixth century a Christian monastic settlement was
established on Inis Cealtra, or Holy Island.*

He's written the book,
ferries travellers there. These days
no money in it
but, *I love it here.* Wind-light
on crimped waves. Mountain-rimmed sky.


Monastic site

A great black-backed gull
presides on high. Mossed crosses.
The Holy Well's lip
against the Shannon's blue gleam.
Portals open to the sky.

St Caimín's Church

A five-inch gap rims
the window-screen. Swallows
fly seamlessly in,
fill beaks, skim the nave, arc out
plotting new geometries.


Tower

Heaped in each window
of the monastery's round tower,
a welter of sticks
like mad wicker-work: ravens
have the best view in Ireland.

## Holy Island

*Bullaun stones, once thought to be warting stones or cursing stones, are now recognised as being grinding stones.*

Grave slabs, bullaun stones.
Archaeologists have asked
the earth their questions.
Yarrow and cuckoo flower grow;
cattle graze; pilgrims still come.


## Five p.m.

A swan family
cutting across the lough – he
of the snarling hiss
bringing up the rear, she spear-
heading six black-eyed wonders.

Evening

A scintillant mass
of starlings rose, turned sideways
on themselves then crashed
like a tidal wave along
the horizon's backlit shore.

Other poetry titles from Clouds of Magellan

**Night Train** by Anthony Lynch

'Anthony Lynch's poetry persuades us into its unique atmosphere, rich with detail ... Meticulous description subtly implicates rather than specifies in these tightly wrought poems that finish unexpectedly, the endings often an entrance to the poem ... a tower of memory that reels back to its origin, to birth, the night train leading into day.'—Gig Ryan

'Lynch's first book of poetry, *Night Train*, contains poetry written with a fine eye for detail and a storyteller's uneasy observations ... His work is subtle, compassionate, eerie ...'—Robyn Rowland, CORDITE

'Lynch does what the best poets do: he inhabits whatever he describes. You feel he has learned something important for himself from Ted Hughes and Sylvia Plath without ignoring William Carlos Williams.'—Kevin Brophy, JACKET2

'*Night Train* takes us on a multifarious journey through the shifting terrain of its poems. The poems never drop into stillness but remain animated. They articulate a contemporary experience of the outer and inner landscape.'—Tina Giannoukos, MASCARA LITERARY REVIEW

Anthony Lynch is a poet, fiction writer, editor and reviewer.

*Electricity for beginners* by Michelle Dicinoski.

Poems about falling in and out of love. Poems about houses that shake and flood. Poems about frisbees and families. Michelle Dicinoski's Electricity for Beginners is a lyrical exploration of the sparks and surges familiar to us all.

'Michelle Dicinoski's poems have that clarity and zest that marks the arrival of a fresh new voice in Australian poetry. She coaxes you into her poems with sweet allure, and keeps you there … This is a book that hums lightly, warmly, and with charmed intimacy.'—Judith Beveridge

'The strength in Michelle Dicinoski's poetry is her faithfulness to gravity and other laws of the physical sciences. But the beauty lies in her bright defiance: celebratory moments in which *the confetti doesn't fall, but floats in place / in the air just beyond us.*'—Bronwyn Lea

**_Now we are four_** by Petrina Barson

_We have a little table_
_for your photo, a candle_
_some objects you lately touched._
_But the whole house has become a shrine ..._

_Now we are four_ is a collection of poems about
intimacy, solitude and family. It charts a journey into
relationship, then the daily life of a small family:
mum, dad, three children—Lara, Maya, Daniel—and
one black dog. The expectation was to create a set of
poems that covered the ordinary luminosity of family
life. But one day, at three-and-a-half years of age,
Maya suddenly died.

'... This is a book of raw and profound poems. They
are not all about Maya, and yet inevitably they are:
the brutal fact of her absence throwing all else into
sharp relief. Early poems evoke the spaciousness
before children—alone and then through the
tentative intimacy of a new relationship—through to
poems on motherhood that exquisitely articulate the
visceral impact of that love. There are poems here
that celebrate joy with an exhilaration that cuts
through any sentimentality this subject risks. Later
poems convey the shattering force of a grief like no
other, the sickening way life carries on while for you
nothing can ever be the same again; and the struggle
to find gratitude for a child's life—no matter how
brief—beyond the terrible pain of loss.'—Rachael
Power, BAREFOOT

**Death in a Swiss zoo** by Mark Wills

*You meet a man for the first time*
*on the last day of his life.*
*He asks if you're keeping busy.*
*Then he and his ruddy cousin*
*talk of a sepia Swan Hill, when 'Cheyenne*
*started at fifty to one, six shillings to win,*
*four bob for us, two bob for mum'.*

This first collection of poems by Melbourne-based
poet Mark Wills is filled with wry observations on
the gap between city and bush, the gap between style
and substance, and tender reflections on intimacy
and family.

Recent fiction from Clouds of Magellan

*Walter* by Ashley Sievwright

Walter Kovak—insurance worker, early forties, unhappily married, no children, memorably invisible—is the sole survivor of a devastating suburban train crash. But Walter has no memory of the tragedy. One year on he starts to receive mysterious random warnings from strangers—warnings that could again save his life. And his memory of the fateful day begins to return.

*All windows open : and other stories* by Hariklia Heristanidis

Chrissie Triantafillou is your average Greek girl growing up in Melbourne in the 1980s. Dark hair, art student, bit of a princess. Other distinguishing features: she has no sense of smell, has been cursed by her mother, and is passionately in love with her cousin George.

Hariklia Heristanidis is a writer and blogger. Her stories open up a world of dreams, desires, and women who either tell fortunes, or—hopefully—make their own.

**Berzoo** by Errol Bray.

*The impact on my body was electric, like someone had stabbed me in the heart with a syringe of adrenalin…*

Berlin, 1995. The Wall is down, Christo has wrapped the Reichstag, and gay travel writer Roger Staines is fast approaching his fortieth birthday. He's experiencing the usual meaning-of-life angst, but things go completely berzoo when he meets Friedrich of the angelic looks, and Nikki of the flaming red hair.

Ricocheting between Sydney, Berlin and Venice, Roger is caught in a world that travel writing didn't prepare him for. Worse still, Roger has learnt how to use a gun and he can't put it down.

'… immensely readable … vivid characterisation, atmospheric Berlin setting, and narrative twists …'
—DNA MAGAZINE

Errol Bray is a playwright; theatre director and dramaturg; founding director of major youth arts projects; and a sometime academic. He is from Sydney, lives in Brisbane, and travels a lot.